THE ART OF GRACEFULLY STANDING UP FOR YOURSELF

WHEN YOU FEEL RUN OVER BY OTHERS

A COACHING HANDBOOK

MICHELE A. TOWERS

ISBN: 1-4537-4517-3

1. Family & Relationships   2. Interpersonal Relations

Scripture quotations in this book are from the Holy Bible: New King James Version,copyright © 1995, 2006 by Thomas Nelson, Inc.
King James Version, copyright © 1999 by Thomas Nelson, Inc. The Message, © 1993 by Eugene H. Peterson New International Version, © 1973, 1978, 1984 by International Bible Society

Edited by Betty J.C. Wright, Carol Gregory and Elaine M. Hansen

Designed by: Shelby Soto, Ingenious Design

Printed in the United States of America

IT ALL STARTED IN THE RESTROOM...

Growing up, I got picked on a lot. I was considered a geek before the word was even popular. Maybe it was because of the coke bottle glasses I wore...or perhaps it was because I got good grades and played in the marching band, like all the other kids in the "geek club". Whatever the reason, I sometimes felt like there was a sign taped to my back that said, "Kick me!"

I'll never forget one incident in middle school. Unbeknownst to me, I had been targeted by the school bully. Before I knew what had happened, I found myself trapped in the girls' restroom by three girls twice my size! The ring-leader (and biggest of them all...) was angry because I had out-jumped her for a jump ball during a basketball game in our 6th hour gym class.

So to save face, she and her cohorts backed me into the corner of the bathroom. She stuck her scowling, menacing face within inches of mine, and gave me a piece of her mind (which as I think back, wasn't much to give).

But I did get the message - if I ever crossed her path again, I would pay dearly for it!

I can't tell you how I managed to get out of there without having the snot beat out of me. All I can say is that I am glad that God is on my side! I did spend the rest of the school year, however, watching my back; afraid that there might be yet another encounter with these horrible bullies.

YOU CAN RUN BUT YOU CAN'T HIDE

That incident in the girls' restroom was just the beginning for me. I did somehow manage to survive middle school, graduated from high school, and eventually graduated from college with a degree in mechanical engineering. Finally, it was time to start my career in corporate America!

Having made it to the professional arena, I figured that things would get easier from there. I thought I was home free! Being a young female in a predominantly male environment, however, I quickly learned how naïve I had been. It didn't take long before I realized that corporate America actually is where the bullies go when they grow up!

I spent years in the workplace afraid…

- Afraid to speak with many of my male co-workers for fear of being ridiculed…

- Afraid to pick up the phone for fear of having to deal with an aggressive field manager…

- Afraid to speak up in meetings for fear of being told I was wrong!

I didn't know how to effectively stand up for myself. For years, I spent every day feeling intimidated; feeling run over by others.

■ ■ ■ ■ ■ ■ ■ ■ ■ ■

Intimidators can show up in any area of your life. Perhaps they sit next to you in the board room; maybe they live next-door; or, they might even be a part of your church volunteer team!

■ ■ ■ ■ ■ ■ ■ ■ ■

Have you ever been pushed around – intimidated – threatened - by someone? The feeling of helplessness can be absolutely paralyzing. Over time, you wind up looking around every corner, afraid of when the next stressful encounter will come.

And unfortunately, intimidation doesn't suddenly vanish just because you grow up. Now that you're an adult, no one is threatening anymore to hang you from your locker or smear gum in your hair. But don't be deceived...the intimidator's methods are now much more sophisticated, but the intentions are the same.

The goal is to keep you quiet. Intimidators want you to remain silent and submissive so that your voice will not – cannot – be heard.

Intimidators can show up in any area of your life. Perhaps they sit next to you in the board room; maybe they live next-door; or, they might even be a part of your church volunteer team!

How many times have you walked away from a situation, stewed on the conversation, and then later thought, "I should have said this…" or "I should have said that…", or "I should have given them a piece of my mind!"?

It can be particularly difficult for "nice people" to stand up for themselves when dealing with bulldozers. "Nice people" tend to be extremely people-oriented and sensitive to the feelings of others.

So what's so wrong with being "nice"?

When a situation arises that requires you to gracefully stand up for yourself, "nice people" find it easier to simply back down. You never want to take the risk of offending another person or creating hurt feelings. Instead, it is safer to leave things unsaid and walk away. You will do whatever is necessary to keep the peace.

But the sad fact is, when you allow yourself to be run over, you will never truly have peace!

And there is an even worse consequence of succumbing to intimidation; when you allow yourself to be run over by others, you then become someone other than your true self.

- You hold back your real thoughts and words for fear of rejection, ridicule or retaliation.

- You become what you think you <u>need</u> to be, other than who you really are.

- Your focus is no longer on thriving, but surviving.

- From that moment on, you are no longer walking in your destiny and purpose.

Another problem with not dealing with strong-willed people is that resentment inevitably escalates. How many times have you walked away from a situation, stewed on the conversation, and then later thought, "I should have said this..." or "I should have said that...", or "I should have given him a piece of my mind!"?

Hours, days, even weeks later, you continue to seethe beneath the surface, angry that you were mistreated. These resentments will eventually come to the surface, perhaps in a way that could cause permanent damage to the relationship.

If you find yourself:

- Easily intimidated by others,
- Not heard by others,
- Not respected by others,
- Allowing others to cross your personal boundaries,

Then it's time to make a change!

In this coaching handbook, we will examine:

- How you are perceived by others, versus how you see yourself,
- Realizing what's really important when dealing with difficult people, and
- How to communicate in a more empowering and confident way.

UNDERSTANDING THE "BULLDOZER"

But let's be careful not to imply that every out-spoken, strong- minded person in your life is "out to get" you.

- Maybe it's simply a well-intended individual who simply isn't aware that he is coming across in an aggressive way.

- Perhaps she is struggling with insecurities of her own and controlling the situation is her only way of protecting herself.

- Perhaps he has good intentions, but just needs to learn to respect others while trying to get the job done.

And we must face the ugly truth; there are others who are just plain 'ole mean. For the purpose of this handbook, we will affectionately refer to these overly-assertive people as "bulldozers". In everyday life, literal bulldozers can be very helpful and useful. However, it's important that they are not allowed to run amuck, or else you're likely to end up with a lot of damage on your hands.

Human bulldozers are very much the same. Often times they mean no harm, but they haven't learned how to communicate in a way that is respectful and productive. Instead, they have a tendency to "bulldoze" their way through life, resulting in weakened relationships.

So, the first matter of business is to adjust your mindset. You can no longer think defensively when it comes to your bulldozer. Make up your mind that you will no longer see yourself as the victim. Remember, the problem you are having may not even be about you, but more about that person. Make a resolution to take the chip off your shoulder as you learn how to deal with the situation in a new and proactive way.

For the purpose of this handbook, we will affectionately refer to these overly-assertive people as "bulldozers".

What to Expect in this Handbook...

This handbook takes a coaching approach to standing up for yourself. My goal is not to give you answers in an exact, specific package. Instead, I recognize that your technique and style are unique, and you will shape your own outcome. You already have the answers within you...you simply need help bringing them out!

This handbook is also not a replacement for one-on-one coaching. I encourage you, after working through this handbook, to continue your work by making an investment in your life by working with a coach. Individualized coaching can help you to work through less obvious issues that may be affecting your ability to gracefully stand up to others. The fieldwork in this handbook is designed to provide you with the groundwork for understanding what you really want from your relationships. They guide you through steps that will assist you in taking new action to get different results.

One final note: This handbook is based on principles from the Bible. I consider the Bible to be the most incredible book ever written when it comes to understanding how to get along well with others. Whatever your belief system, this timeless book can provide you with an incredible source of insight and advice on how to be a winner in life!

I have always been compelled by a specific scripture in the book of Matthew. It states, "**...So be as shrewd as snakes and harmless as doves" (Matthew 10:16, NIV).**

This means that when dealing with others, we shouldn't be naïve; instead, we should be totally aware of who and what we are dealing with. We are not to walk into any situation unguarded or ignorant. Instead, we are to go in with our eyes wide open, understanding exactly who and what we are dealing with.

At the same time, we are not to allow the situation or environment to adversely affect how we respond to others. We are to be respectful and honorable in all situations and at all times. It is never okay to be rude, unkind or nasty to others. To sum it up, we are to be strong and smart when it comes to dealing with others; while exhibiting graciousness and gentleness.

"...So be as shrewd as snakes and harmless as doves."(Matthew 10:16)

This handbook will not teach you how to put your bulldozer "in his place", or to demean him in any way. Instead, it is intended to help you become more aware of the traps you fall into with your bulldozer. You will learn to stand strong, while exhibiting grace and kindness.

Keep this Matthew 10:16, NIV. scripture in your mind as you work through the process. It will help you maintain a healthy balance of strength and grace while learning to stand up to your bulldozer.

So, if you are ready... let's get started!

A SNAPSHOT OF TODAY

Before changing any situation, it is always important to take a close, honest look at where you are today. Let's start by gathering some essential information:

FIELD WORK:

Take a moment to think of the relationship where you face a bulldozer. Who is this person? In what environment do youencounter him/her?

_____

_____

Try to recall the last difficult conversation you had with this person. What was the discussion about?

_____

_____

_____

_____

_____

On a scale from 1 to 10, how successful was this conversation? _____

As you think back on this conversation, what part of it was disappointing to you?

_____

_____

_____

_____

How did this make you feel?

_____

_____

_____

What would you like to have done or said differently to give you a better result?

_____

_____

_____

_____

_____

_____

_____

How do you believe this would have changed the outcome?

_____

_____

_____

_____

How would you feel differently about yourself, had the outcome been the way you envision?

_____

_____

_____

It will require some work – and probably some tension - to bring about the change that you want. Are you willing to face discomfort to have the change you want?

_____

If your answer is "no" to the last question, then you might want to set this handbook aside until you are ready for this challenge. Don't be hard on yourself – you will know when the time is right. But I want to ask you; what's stopping you?

If your answer is "yes", I want to say "Congratulations!" You have made an important decision to begin changing your life for the better!

Now, let's move on...

We all have certain relational qualities that send out messages to those we spend time with. Your relational qualities determine the "vibe" you send out to others.

Some people exude confidence and leadership; some others have the uncanny ability to confirm that you are appreciated and loved. Others have a way of creating excitement and enthusiasm whenever they are around.

On the other side of the coin, some people leave you feeling drained after a conversation. And there are still others who tend to leave you feeling stressed out and tense after spending time with them.

So the question is, **what relational "vibe" are you projecting?**

Before answering that question, consider this:

How you believe you come across to others may be quite different from how others actually perceive you.

Here's what I mean:

I once coached a client – we'll call her Chris - who wanted to make a career shift. In her work environment Chris was well respected, trusted and liked. She was responsible for making major decisions every day. There were many people who not only reported to her, but looked to her for leadership, direction and instruction.

Chris succeeded in everything she put her hands to, and she did her job very well!

Not far into our sessions, she realized that her self-perception did not align with how others perceived her. In spite of her personal success, Chris was blind to her own strengths and abilities. While others saw her relational quality as confident, she identified with weakness. While others saw her relational quality as firm and decisive, she perceived herself as indecisive and unsure.

Chris soon realized that it was actually okay for her to acknowledge and embrace her gifts and abilities. And with a realistic and accurate view of her true self, she was able to achieve inner confidence!

How you believe you come across to others may be quite different from how others actually perceive you.

Here is another example:

Another client of mine – we'll call her Jan - couldn't understand why she had a difficult time getting ahead on her job. Although Jan is a wonderfully sweet woman, she is also the first to admit that she has a very direct style of communication. She recognized that people often misunderstood her good intentions, and this at times has blocked her success.

During one of our sessions, Jan told me about a conversation she had with her boss earlier that day. This discussion had taken a turn south, ending in frustration for both of them. I asked her to replay the conversation to me. As she recited the verbal exchange from earlier that day, she suddenly realized where she had gone wrong...

Jan saw she had come across like a bulldozer! Without her even realizing it, her relational quality had been aggressive, reflected by her body language and choice of words.

Jan's perceived relational qualities hadn't matched up with what she was actually projecting. Throughout the rest of our session, we worked together to develop a plan for a softer approach, giving her a better outcome in the future.

You are not always the best judge of your own relational qualities. Being so close to yourself, it's often difficult to see the forest for the trees. Perhaps you underestimate yourself by not recognizing a certain skill or quality. Or it's possible that you may have a blind spot that is hindering you without your even knowing it.

This next exercise will help you discover your true relational qualities.

FIELD WORK:

This next exercise will help you discover your relational qualities, particularly when dealing with your bulldozer.

Look over this list of relational qualities and circle the seven that you believe most represent you when relating to your bulldozer.

Consider, when around your bulldozer, what's happening with you:

- How do you behave?
- How do you feel?
- How do you sound?
- What are you thinking?

Keep in mind that this is not a test...there is no right or wrong answer. Don't select characteristics that you wish you had. Don't avoid characteristics that you wish you didn't have. Rather, give yourself the freedom to simply be totally honest and transparent.

Now, go for it!

Focused on self	Candid	Focused	Wishy-washy
Good listener	Cheerful	Friendly	Humble
Combative	Lacks confidence	Honest	Stubborn
Goal-oriented	Realistic	Unresponsive	Too open-minded
Pessimistic	Grouchy	Trusting	Calm
Flexible	Guarded	Direct	Yielding
Caring	Confident	Suspicious of Others	Considerate
Cooperative	Decisive	Unsure of goals	Dislikes Change
Excited	Nervous	Strong	Tired
Brave	Fearful	Positive attitude	Emotional
Guarded	Wavering	Naïve	Blunt
Comfortable	Other:	Other:	Other:

Look over your choices and write them down, with (1) being the most prominent and (7) being the least prominent:

1. _____

2. _____

3. _____

4. _____

5. _____

6. _____

7. _____

Great job! You have just summarized your self-perceived relational qualities. Chances are that there are positive qualities on the list, as well as some you would like to work on eliminating. Don't worry about that – we'll get to that later.

And now it's time to take this exercise one step further...

FIELD WORK:

The next important step is to identify the relational qualities that <u>others</u> see in you.

Select <u>two people whom you trust</u> to help you with this field work. These should be people who see you interact with your bulldozer on a regular basis. They should be individuals who:

- are confidential,
- are willing to tell you the truth, and
- Sincerely want you to succeed.

Once again, it is very helpful if the people you have selected have seen you "in action" with your bulldozer. Having seen how you and your bulldozer relate to each other, your trusted friends will have valuable input that will help you improve in this area.

Tear out the following two blank forms, and give each of your friends a copy of the same exercise you just completed. Ask them to complete the exercises to help you identify your prominent relational qualities. When going through this process, they should consider which qualities most accurately represent **YOU**.

Have them complete the page, and then return it to you.

Thank you for taking the time to contribute to my personal growth!

I selected you for these exercises because I know without a shadow of a doubt that you are confidential, willing to tell me the truth, with a desire to see me succeed. So I'm giving you permission to be totally honest and transparent.

Please look over this list of relational qualities and circle the seven that you believe most represent me when relating to _____ (Name the bulldozer).

When selecting the qualities that represent me, consider:

- How do I behave when dealing with this person?
- How do I sound when dealing with this person?
- What body language do I demonstrate when dealing with this person?

Focused on self	Candid	Focused	Wishy-washy
Good listener	Cheerful	Friendly	Humble
Combative	Lacks confidence	Honest	Stubborn
Goal-oriented	Realistic	Unresponsive	Too open-minded
Pessimistic	Grouchy	Trusting	Calm
Flexible	Guarded	Direct	Yielding
Caring	Confident	Suspicious of Others	Considerate

Cooperative	Decisive	Unsure of goals	Dislikes Change
Excited	Nervous	Strong	Tired
Brave	Fearful	Positive attitude	Emotional
Guarded	Wavering	Naïve	Blunt
Comfortable	Other:	Other:	Other:

Take a look at your choices and write them down, with (1) being the most prominent and (7) being the least prominent:

1. _____

2. _____

3. _____

4. _____

5. _____

6. _____

7. _____

Please return this to me. Thank you again for your invaluable input!

Thank you for taking the time to contribute to my personal growth!

I selected you for these exercises because I know without a shadow of a doubt that you are confidential, willing to tell me the truth, with a desire to see me succeed. So I'm giving you permission to be totally honest and transparent.

Please look over this list of relational qualities and circle the seven that you believe most represent me when relating to _____ (Name the bulldozer).

When selecting the qualities that represent me, consider:

- How do I behave when dealing with this person?
- How do I sound when dealing with this person?
- What body language do I demonstrate when dealing with this person?

Focused on self	Candid	Focused	Wishy-washy
Good listener	Cheerful	Friendly	Humble
Combative	Lacks confidence	Honest	Stubborn
Goal-oriented	Realistic	Unresponsive	Too open-minded
Pessimistic	Grouchy	Trusting	Calm
Flexible	Guarded	Direct	Yielding
Caring	Confident	Suspicious of Others	Considerate

Cooperative	Decisive	Unsure of goals	Dislikes Change
Excited	Nervous	Strong	Tired
Brave	Fearful	Positive attitude	Emotional
Guarded	Wavering	Naïve	Blunt
Comfortable	Other:	Other:	Other:

Take a look at your choices and write them down, with (1) being the most prominent and (7) being the least prominent:

1. _____

2. _____

3. _____

4. _____

5. _____

6. _____

7. _____

Please return this to me. Thank you again for your invaluable input!

Now that you have received honest feedback from trustworthy sources, it's time to compare their perceptions to your own.

FIELD WORK:

When comparing your friends' list to your own, what relational qualities did you find in common?

_____

_____

What does this confirm about you?

_____

_____

_____

Which relational qualities do you have on your list that your friends did not?

_____

_____

How does your personal self-perception differ from how your friends see you?

_____

_____

_____

Which relational qualities did your friends list that you did not?

_____

_____

Is it possible that you have a blind spot concerning this area?

_____

_____

What perceptions of yourself might you need to change?

_____

_____

_____

What have you learned about yourself as a result of this exercise?

_____

_____

_____

Congratulations on completing Step 1, "Taking a Snapshot of Today"! You now have a more clear and accurate understanding of your personal relational qualities.

You have successfully identified – and hopefully embraced - your relational strengths. Celebrate them!

You also have a better idea of certain relational qualities you need to work on. Now that you have taken action to identify them, you are on your way to overcoming them!

Next, it's time to think about what you really <u>want</u> from your bulldozer relationship...

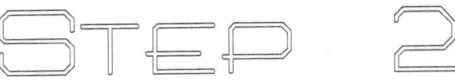

STEP 2

Whether you are aware of it or not, you have a personal motive for every relationship in your life.

Think about it...you marry because you _desire_ to share your life with someone. You build friendships because you _need_ trusting and fun interaction with others. You get to know your neighbors because you _want_ to have a support system in your community.

Every relationship - whether it is personal, professional or social - has a desire, need, or want attached to it. And the type of relationship you are in determines what you really want from that connection.

███████████

Whether you are aware of it or not, you have a personal motive for every relationship in your life.

███████████

For example, let's assume that your job requires you to collaborate with others in order to complete certain projects. Although it would be great to develop long-lasting relationships with co- workers, friendship will probably not be the most important motive in that environment. What's really important is creating a level of cooperation and team work so that you can get your job done.

31

On the other hand, relationships with family members and close friends will stem from different motives. For people with whom you have a personal investment, your motive is to create and sustain a foundation of love, respect and trust for healthy relationships. Here are just a few of the wants, needs or desires that shape and drive our relationships:

1. **Respect** – You treat each other with honor.
2. **Friendship** – There are shared experiences between you.
3. **Trust** – You share a safe and open environment.
4. **Cooperation** – You work well together.
5. **Results** – You are able to get things done when working together.
6. **Love** – You treat each other with patience, kindness and goodness.
7. **Enjoyment** – You like spending time with each other.
8. **Appreciation** – You acknowledge each other's value and uniqueness.

YOU CAN'T HAVE IT ALL

You should understand your primary purpose for every relationship in your life. Once you know what you want, need or desire from the relationship, it will help you stay focused on the issues that are most important.

This brings me to an important point. One of the greatest obstacles that "nice people" must get past is the fear of upsetting others. I have heard from countless numbers of "nice people":

- "I don't want her to be angry at me!"
- "What if he doesn't speak to me anymore?"
- "I don't want to hurt his feelings!"

Which leads us to a critical point:

DISAGREEMENT DOES NOT EQUATE TO MEANNESS

Disagreement is perfectly normal. It is a part of every relationship and a part of life. Disagreements cause us to grow, consider new ideas and become more tolerant of others. It offers opportunity for honesty and forgiveness. Disagreement does not have to destroy your relationship. In fact, it can potentially take it to a more meaningful level!

If your primary motive is to "keep the peace" between you and your bulldozer, you will never be empowered to gracefully stand up for yourself. You must dispel the fear of upsetting your bulldozer! Resign yourself to the fact that things might have to get worse between you and your bulldozer before it gets better. But ask yourself if it is worth the cost to gain what you really want, need or desire.

It is also important to acknowledge the possibility that your bulldozer may not share your wants, needs and desires for the relationship.

The hard truth is that your bulldozer may not be the least bit interested in becoming your friend. She may not be personally capable of giving you the positive feedback you need. She might have a trust issue, and may always be suspicious of you and your motives.

33

Don't take this response personally. As we considered earlier, your bulldozer might have personal issues that have absolutely nothing to do with you. Instead of allowing yourself to become hurt or offended, set your goal on building a relationship that works for both of you.

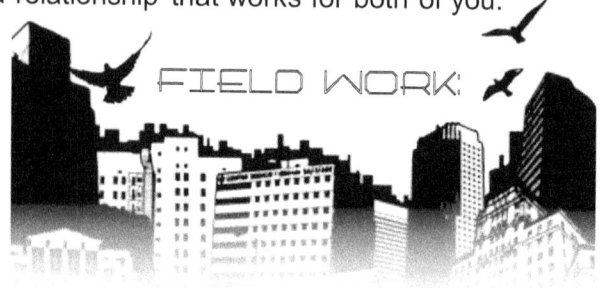

FIELD WORK:

Decide which wants, needs or desires mentioned above are most important in the relationship with your bulldozer. Which three MUST you have in order for this relationship to be successful? Feel free to add others if what you need are not listed.

1. _____
2. _____
3. _____

THE FOUNDATIONAL MOTIVE

I can't resist providing you with a "hint": I hope that somewhere on your short list, "respect" shows up. The Bible says that "A woman of gentle grace gets **respect**..." (Proverbs 11:16, The Message). Respect is the foundation of every strong relationship. All other wants, needs and desires are built upon the foundation of respect.

- If respect is absent, love is not genuine.
- If respect is absent, appreciation will also be lacking.
- If respect is absent, trust cannot be fully developed.

All healthy relationships are foundation on <u>respect</u>, so make sure that it shows up on your list.

Now that you have determined your primary wants, needs and desires from your bulldozer, consider these questions:

Respect is the foundation of every strong relationship. All other wants, needs and desires are built upon the foundation of respect.

Have you had any unrealistic/misdirected wants, needs or desires in the relationship with your bulldozer?What are they?

_____

_____

_____

What wants, needs or desires are you willing to let go of in this relationship?

_____

_____

What wants, needs or desires will you insist on that were not present before?

_____

_____

_____

_____

How will the relationship change by re-prioritizing your wants, needs and desires?

_____

_____

_____

_____

Who do you need to be to help raise the relationship to this level?

_____

_____

_____

_____

_____

You have just completed Step 2, "Understanding What You Really Want"...Great job!

Now that you have established some important truths about who you are and what is really important for you, it's time to move on to the next step – "Preparing for the Conversation".

STEP 3

Here is another common mistake that "nice people" make when dealing with their bulldozer:

You hope that the next time – miraculously – perhaps you will be able to have a constructive, non-confrontational encounter with your bulldozer. The hope of all "nice people" is that eventually everyone can walk hand in hand, with cooperation and respect.

"Nice people" are eternal optimist, always willing to give others the benefit of the doubt! Optimism and graciousness are amazing and wonderful qualities to have. However, consider the words of Albert Einstein who said, "The definition of insanity is doing the same thing over and over again and expecting different results".

If the approach you have used in the past hasn't worked for you, it's time to try something different. And that something is to make a plan!

Before a basketball team enters a game, they prepare for their opponent. They study the other team's strengths and weaknesses. They take an honest look at their own performance and decide what changes they need to make to shore up the chinks in their own armor. Based on what they see, they then develop a plan of action that will give them their desired outcome – a win!

Similarly, in order to have a meaningful and constructive relationship with your bulldozer, you must first develop a thoughtful plan that will get you the results you want.

Respect is the foundation of every strong relationship. All other wants, needs and desires are built upon the foundation of respect.

KNOW WHO YOU'RE DEALING WITH

It is important to keep in mind that everyone is different.

- Everyone has a unique way of communicating.
- Everyone has a unique way of processing information.
- Everyone has a unique way of getting things done.

Understanding your personality type as well as that of your bulldozer can help you develop an approach that will give you more positive results.

For example, let's say that your bulldozer is the "no-nonsense" type who is very direct and to the point. In this case, you will need to use a direct approach.

Don't engage your bulldozer without first having your facts in order. Don't become too emotional. Don't beat around the bush when making your point. Instead, be prepared to say exactly what you mean. Be prepared to remain calm, cool and collected. Just be prepared.

On the other hand, some bulldozers may put a high priority on relationships and friendships. In this case, you will need to approach them in a relational way. Don't overlook him as a person. Don't be too quick to get down to business. Don't be blunt when talking with him. Instead, take some time to ask how his weekend was. Ask how his children are doing. Ask how he is doing, and allow time for a thoughtful answer.

The first key to developing your game plan is to try understanding where your bulldozer is coming from. Then consider how you can adjust your approach in a way that produces a winning conversation.

FIELD WORK:

What do you know about your bulldozer's method of communicating?

_____

_____

_____

_____

_____

How does this differ from your way of communicating?

_____

_____

What do you know about how your bulldozer processes information?

_____

_____

How does this differ from how you process information?

_____

_____

What do you know about how your bulldozer likes to get things done?

_____

_____

How does this differ from your way of getting things done?

_____

_____

In what ways can you adjust your overall approach that will improve how you and your bulldozer interact?

_____

_____

_____

Once you are able to tap into the secret of effectively relating to another's personality, you will find that relationships in all areas of your life can improve almost instantly!

There are many personality assessment tools out there on the market. I am most impressed with the Peoplemap™ system developed by Dr. E. Michael Lillibridge." Not only is this system extremely accurate and very simple, but it is also inexpensive relative to some other assessment tools.

If you would like to learn more about personality styles using the Peoplemap™ system, you are invited to visit my website at:

www.strongtowercoaching.com

EXPECT CONFLICT

For the time being, whenever you interact with your bulldozer, decide that you will be prepared for potential conflict!

I know…As a "nice person", I'll bet you are cringing in your seat right about now. Most "nice people" would rather go under the dentist's drill before facing conflict! But to prevent being caught off guard, it's a good idea to hope for the best but prepare for the worst.

It's vital that you overcome your apprehension about disputing your bulldozer. To get you started, let's examine how you perceive conflict:

Respect is the foundation of every strong relationship. All other wants, needs and desires are built upon the foundation of respect.

FIELD WORK:

In your own words, how do you define conflict?

_____

_____

_____

When it comes to conflict, what are you really afraid of?

_____

_____

_____

Do you think your fear may be realistic, or exaggerated?

_____

_____

_____

Are you willing to risk conflict with your bulldozer to get what you really need from this relationship?

_____

_____

_____

The dictionary defines conflict is as follows:

"To come into collision or disagreement; be contradictory, at variance, or in opposition; clash: The account of one eyewitness conflicted with that of the other." (The American Heritage® Dictionary of the English Language, Fourth Edition Copyright © 2006 by Houghton Mifflin Company.

How could this definition work in a positive way to strengthen the relationship between you and your bulldozer?

_____

_____

_____

Keeping this in mind, what's the best outcome you could gain if or when conflict arises with your bulldozer?

_____

_____

_____

Facing conflict might never become comfortable. It may never be easy or feel natural. However, it can lead to honest discussion, and ultimately a stronger and better relationship. Conflict in itself is not a bad thing

As you change and begin to gracefully stand up for yourself, you are inviting the potential for conflict. After all, you are basically saying, "No, I'm not going to take this from you anymore". Don't be surprised if your newly-found strength is met with resistance.

By the way, anticipating conflict doesn't equate to being aggressive or angry towards your bulldozer. It doesn't mean that you should walk into the conversation with a chip on your shoulder.

Adopt a positive attitude about conflict. This will empower you to walk into any situation calm, cool, collected, and ready for anything. You will make it clear that you are finished with getting run over, but you'll do it with kindness and respect.

Don't be surprised if your newly- found strength is met with resistance.

Another important step to preparing to face your bulldozer is to laser in on what you want from that specific discussion. A female client of mine (Bev) works in a work environment that is predominantly male. She was responsible for completing a project but was having a tough time getting her subordinates to meet their deadlines. As we worked together to help her prepare for her next encounter with her subordinates, Bev discovered something that blocked her from getting what she needed.

Whenever Bev approached these guys with questions concerning their completion dates, they gave a thousand reasons why they couldn't meet her deadline. She was continuously drawn into discussions about all the other work they had do. The more she listened, the guiltier she felt for putting pressure on them. As a result, she regularly backed down from what she needed, creating doubt in her supervisor's mind about her ability to get the job done.

Their tactic of leading Bev down bunny trails had worked – that is, until she began to stay focused on the task at hand. We role played to practice for their next conversation. She rehearsed statements like;

"I completely understand that you have a lot on your plate right now, but this is important too. How can we come up with a solution that will work for all of us?" and, *"What obstacle can I help you remove that will help us meet our deadline?"*

47

Don't allow yourself to take the bait of the bunny trail. That will only result in confusion, complication and frustration. No matter what, stay focused on what's important.

FIELD WORK:

As you prepare for your next conversation, what outcomes do you desire?

_____

_____

_____

Have you been led down bunny trails in the past? How did it affect your outcome?

_____

_____

_____

How can you approach your next conversation differently to stay focused on what you need?

_____

_____

_____

After a conversation with your bulldozer, have you ever said...?

"Once I got home, I thought of a great come back!"

"I really should have said..."

"I wish I had thought of that during our conversation!"

"If I had it to do over again, I would say..."

It seems that in the heat of the moment, it's sometimes difficult to come up with the right response to an objection or challenge. But this is a skill that can be learned, with a little practice.

I have a pet name for my dear husband, George...I lovingly call him "The Sniper". George has no fear when it comes to dealing with difficult people. If a bulldozer feels bold enough to hurl a sarcastic remark in his direction, he kicks into action! Like a sniper, he aims shoots and strikes right between the eyes with the perfect response. And as with an expert marksman nestled in the bushes, you never even see the shot coming!

It's actually very impressive to see him in action...

What's even more impressive is that he is able to respond in a way that is not only strong, but respectful and tactful. He is never insulting, and in fact often addresses his bulldozer with a touch of humor. But one thing is very clear; he's not about to allow anyone to run over him!

Being married to "The Sniper" has taught me something; it helps to have a ready response when dealing with your bulldozer.

Proverbs 15:28 says, "The heart of the righteous studies how to answer, but the mouth of the wicked pours forth evil" (NIV).

It seems that in the heat of the moment, it's sometimes difficult to come up with the right response to an objection or challenge. But this is a skill that can be learned, with a little practice.

It is wise to prepare yourself for potential objections. Your ability to respond to whatever your bulldozer throws at you helps you maintain an air of strength and confidence during your conversation.

For starters, here are a few examples of helpful responses when you are at a loss for words:

- "That's not going to work for me right now"
- "I don't think so"
- "I need to know how you're going to handle this"
- "We're getting off track by talking about this right now"
- "I understand your frustration, but that's the way it is right now."

- *"I appreciate your input, but I feel I have a handle on this right now."*
- *How can I help you remove the obstacle so we can move forward?"*
- *"This is not about you or me. This is about what's best for the customers (or the children, or the team, etc.)."*

Don't fall into the trap of feeling obligated to explain yourself to your bulldozer. Having to explain yourself puts you on the defensive. Not only that, but it also leads you down that endless bunny trail to nowhere. You don't have to provide a long explanatory response. You are not obliged to explain <u>why</u> you feel a particular way. You don't need to share information your bulldozer doesn't need to know. You shouldn't have to defend your feelings or thoughts. Keep your responses succinct and clear.

When relating with your bulldozer, keep in mind that sometimes, less is more.

FIELD WORK:

Thinking back on past conversations, what comments has your bulldozer consistently thrown at you that have left you speechless?

_____

_____

Develop two or three responses you believe will be helpful when confronted by your bulldozer. Feel free to adopt or adjust one of the examples above, or better yet, create your own.

1. _____

2. _____

3. _____

Great job! You have just completed Step 3, "Preparing for the Conversation"! So far,

- You have successfully taken a hard, honest look at where you are today;

- You understand clearly what you want and expect from this relationship; and

- You are prepared for your next conversation with your bulldozer.

Once again, I want to congratulate you for your hard work! Now, it's time to take all you've learned and put it into action!

STEP 4

Now you are fully equipped and armed to engage your bulldozer in power, strength and compassion!

There is no need to be nervous. You have no reason to feel apprehensive. Your intention all along has been to create a positive and healthy relationship. So, remember that "Goodness" is on your side!

One of my favorite Bible scriptures is, "For God hath not given us the spirit of fear, but of power and of love and of a sound mind" (2 Timothy 1:7, KJV). You no longer have to operate out of fear; but you can allow love, good intention, and clarity to motivate your thoughts and actions!

There is no need to be nervous. You have no reason to feel apprehensive. Your intention all along has been to create a positive and healthy relationship, so remember that "Goodness" is on your side! .

If there is a specific issue you need to deal with, it is important to schedule time to meet with your bulldozer. This need not be a formal meeting, but it best to talk during a time that works well for both of you. Resist the temptation to stop her in the hallway to address your issues. Instead, you might even want to give her a heads up about what you want to talk about, so she doesn't feel blind- sighted.

Here's another thought; have you noticed that some people tend to be easier to talk with over the phone than in person, while others are easier to deal with in person versus over the phone?

My husband works with a man - we'll call him John. John is generally a good guy. However, whenever George talks with him over the phone, John tends to be extremely abrupt, abrasive and impatient. In spite of my husband's efforts to lighten his mood and "warm him up", John continues to send the message that he has no desire to cooperate, and would rather be left alone.

So, my husband usually ends up going to see him in person. The moment he sets foot into John's office, John's whole demeanor changes! No longer is he grouchy and in a rush, but he is pleasant! "How's it going, George?" "It's good to see you!" With face-to-face interaction, John becomes cooperative and much easier to deal with.

FIELD WORK:

In what settings have you found your bulldozer to be the most amiable?

_____

_____

In what setting have you found your bulldozer to be the least cooperative?

_____

_____

How can you use this awareness to your advantage?

_____

_____

Email has many useful purposes, but dealing with conflict is not one of those times! So unless there is information you absolutely need to document or confirm, don't hide behind emails.

Until you no longer feel intimidated by your bulldozer, it is best to speak with your bulldozer in person. Make a point to talk to your bulldozer face-to-face or on the phone as much as possible until you feel you have established the kind of relationship you want.

For the most part, now is not the time to use email. Your bulldozer needs to hear the confidence in your voice. She needs to hear your sincerity. She needs to know that you are not afraid to deal with her one-on-one.

Email has many useful purposes (we'll cover that later on), but dealing with conflict is not one of those times! So unless there is information you absolutely need to document or confirm, don't hide behind emails. Instead, show your bulldozer that you are standing up for yourself – face to face!

DURING THE CONVERSATION

Okay, the moment of truth has arrived and the two of you are ready to talk! These exercises will help you during the conversation:

FIELD WORK:

1. Keep your emotions in check. This is a big one for many "nice people".

Don't take what is said personally. Remember, bulldozers have their own set of issues and problems. The way bulldozers respond often says more about what they are struggling with internally; chances are this is not even about you! Don't allow bulldozers to accuse you of being overly emotional. Try hard to keep your voice steady, strong and calm.

Is this an area you personally need to develop? Why or why not?

_____

_____

_____

2. Use appropriate facial expressions. When talking with your bulldozer, make sure that your facial expressions match what you are saying. When making a strong, serious statement, don't crush your credibility by smiling inappropriately. It may be tempting to try softening your words with a grin or nervous laughter, but this will only confuse the issue. You want your bulldozer to be very clear that you are serious. So be sure that your facial expressions align with your words.

Is this an area you personally need to develop? Why or why not?

_____

_____

_____

3. <u>Maintain eye contact.</u> When in a difficult conversation, you can quickly give away your confidence by constantly looking away. Be sure to keep your eye contact steady and strong the entire time.

Is this an area you personally need to develop? Why or why not?

_____

_____

_____

_____

4. <u>Don't ask. Tell.</u> If you need something from your bulldozer, make it very clear. Be careful not to pose your requirement in the form of a question, but tell her exactly what you need. For example, instead of "Janet, would you be able to organize the data for me?" you want to say, "Janet, I need you to organize that data for me".

Is this an area you personally need to develop? Why or why not?

_____

_____

_____

_____

5. <u>Allow for silence.</u> It's not necessary to fill every second with talking. If silence finds its way into the conversation, don't freak out and start filling the space with words. Silence, in fact, can be a very powerful way of communicating. So don't resist silence, but allow it to work for you.

Is this an area you personally need to develop? Why or why not?

_____

_____

6. <u>Balance strength with compassion.</u> Make a point to acknowledge your bulldozer's position. Make sure that she knows that she has been heard. At the same time, stay focused on your goal and don't back down at the first sign of resistance.

Is this an area you personally need to develop? Why or why not?

_____

_____

You have worked hard to get to this point. And remember that you are fully equipped to face your bulldozer with confidence, grace and strength.

You have successfully completed Step 4, "The Rubber Hits the Road". You are now ready to face your bulldozer. So, what are you waiting for? Go for it!

STEP 5

TIME FOR EVALUATION

You did it!

Congratulations on dealing with your bulldozer head on! What you have accomplished is no easy task, and you should take a moment to pat yourself on the back for a job well done!

Now, it is time to take a look at how you did.

FIELD WORK:

What did you do or say differently this time that worked well for you?

_____

_____

_____

How do you believe this changed the outcome?

_____

_____

_____

How did this make you feel?

_____

_____

On a scale from 1 to 10, how successful do you feel this conversation was? ___

Compare this score to the one you gave yourself at the beginning of this handbook. Have you made an improvement?

_____

_____

What can you do differently the next time to make your interaction even better?

_____

_____

Learning to gracefully stand up for yourself is a process. It will take time, and you will only get better the more you practice these principles. So don't be hard on yourself if you didn't handle yourself perfectly. Applaud yourself for your development, and decide what areas of growth you will continue to work on!

Learning to gracefully stand up for yourself is a process. It will take time, and you will only get better the more you practice these principles.

You have made a wonderful start to building a healthier relationship with your bulldozer. So to solidify the gains you have made, be sure to follow up.

Emails can be a very effective way of following-up, and can serve many purposes:

- They can document what was said in a conversation, so that facts don't get confused down the road.

- They can be a means of including others who need to be informed of what's going on.

- They can be a way of clarifying expectations or "next steps"

- They can be used to document another person's good work and efforts, creating a foundation of trust.

Depending on how the meeting with your bulldozer turned out, your follow up will vary.

IF THINGS WENT WELL...

If your bulldozer is in your work environment, you might want to follow up your conversation with an email.

1. First thank your bulldozer for taking the time to talk with you. Then let him know that you appreciate his work, input or ideas. Share with him that he is a valuable part of the team.

2. Restate any important points that the two of you discussed during your talk.   Remind him of any commitments you or he made during your conversation.

3. Make a point of telling him in the email how he made a positive contribution.   CC his manager or supervisor. This is a sure-fire way to build trust and a sense of partnership.

If your situation is not business-related but personal, you might want to consider sending a card, an e-card or even a gift. Let your bulldozer know how much you appreciate him.   Affirm him by sharing a positive quality that you notice about him.

FIELD WORK:

Before sending your   official follow-up   email, construct a practice email or card.   After writing it, set it aside for a while and then come back to it.   Make any changes you think are needed before officially sending it out.

_____

_____

_____

_____

_____

_____

_____

_____

IF THINGS DIDN'T GO SO WELL...

I sincerely hope that your conversation went smoothly without any bumps or opposition. But there is a chance that your bulldozer put up a bit of a fight. Perhaps he didn't want to cooperate. Maybe he didn't want to listen to your side. Or maybe he was just plan disrespectful. What do you do <u>now?</u>

Now is the time to reinforce your stand!

As before, you will want to follow up your conversation with an email.

1. First thank your bulldozer for taking the time to talk with you. Then let him know that you appreciate his work, input or ideas. Share with him that he is a valuable part of the team.

2. Next, clarify the problem, its importance, and the consequences if a solution is not found. Let him know that you are willing to help in whatever way you can.

3. Remind him of any commitments you or he made during your conversation. If you made a request that

was not acknowledged during your conversation, clearly restate your request in the email.

4. Offer any solutions you might have. Ask for input. Let him know you would like to get this resolved quickly.

5. End on a positive note by reminding him that you appreciate him.

Before sending your official follow-up email, construct a practice email or card. After writing it, set it aside for a while and then come back to it. Make any changes you think are needed before officially sending it out.

_____

_____

_____

_____

_____

_____

_____

_____

IF THAT DOESN'T WORK...

If after sending out your email you still don't get the cooperation you need, it is time to escalate the matter. Resend the email, stating that it is imperative that this matter be taken care of. And cc his boss or supervisor.

If you are like most "nice people", the idea of cc'ing a higher-up can be frightening! But this step is critical if you want to gain the respect of your bulldozer.

You're goal is not to get anyone in trouble. Your goal is to get the job done. Eventually your bulldozer will recognize that you are no longer afraid. He will understand that it's not okay to take advantage of you any longer. He will begin to see that you have changed, and he will need to change how he responds to you from now on.

If you are like most "nice people", the idea of cc'ing a higher-up can be frightening! But this step is critical if you want to gain the respect of your bulldozer.

STEP 6

You should be incredibly proud of yourself for taking this journey! Learning to gracefully stand up for yourself has required honesty, open-mindedness and courage on your part. As you made the decision to begin standing up for yourself, you have made a commitment to YOU - - to learn, practice, grow, and most importantly – always respect yourself!

So, where do you go from here?

First, don't be surprised or disappointed if your bulldozer doesn't change right away. Remember that she has become accustomed to relating to you in a certain manner, and it will take some time for her to realize that the rules have changed. Whenever you strive to create change, you will always encounter resistance. Resistance doesn't indicate that you are wrong in trying to change things. Rather, it is a natural part of change. Don't give up. Keep in mind that **resistance requires persistence!**

Don't be surprised if your bulldozer is angry at you for a while. This is sometimes part of the process when you make up your mind that you will no longer be run over. Keep in mind that for this season in your life, it may be more important to be respected than liked. Things can eventually turn for the better between you and your bulldozer, if you are willing to persevere.

Make a commitment to continually treat your bulldozer with respect during the process. Ensure that you listen to her, let her know that she is being heard, and acknowledge the good in her. Eventually she will come around, and your relationship will be stronger and healthier than ever!

Resistance doesn't indicate that you are wrong in trying to change things. Rather, it is a natural part of change. Don't give up.

IS IT TIME TO SAY GOODBYE?

But let's face the facts – regardless of how hard you try, some people are determined to remain "stuck" where they are, refusing to change or grow. That's when it's time for you to make some personal decisions. There may come a day when you will have to make some tough choices.

If your continued efforts to build a relationship of respect and care are rejected, you may have to consider limiting your association with your bulldozer. After all, your health and well- being is ultimately most important.

If your bulldozer is a friend, it _may_ be time to consider removing yourself from the friendship. If your bulldozer is a boss, it maybe time to look for another job. If your bulldozer is a co-worker, it _may_ be time to stop going to lunch together and restrict your interaction to "work only".

Dealing with family, however, is not so simple. You may not be able to physically remove yourself from your bulldozer. And in the case of family, make up your mind to try all possibilities before giving up on your bulldozer! The Bible says, "...love covers over a multitude of sins" (I Peter 4:8, NIV). I personally believe that this applies even more so for family. There are ways, however, to protect yourself from a bulldozer in your family who refuses to change. It doesn't require abandonment. It doesn't require divorce. It doesn't require contention. It simply requires a change in your thinking.

Many years ago, I was speaking with the pastor of the church I was attending at that time. I was sharing with him that I felt unappreciated by my husband, George.

Well actually, when I think back on it, I was whining.

I was complaining about how I felt ignored; how George didn't do this; how George never said that...you get the idea. I'll never forget what that pastor said. When I had finally finished my laundry list of disappointments, he looked at me and simply said, "Lower your expectations". Then he walked out of the room.

What this experience taught me is that we cannot always change how others behave, but we DO have the power to change how situations affect us.

- Do you need to change the expectations you have put on your bulldozer?

- Do you need to remove expectations from your bulldozer if they are not able to meet those expectations?

- Do you need to create an "invisible barrier" around your emotions when around your bulldozer?

You may not have the power to change the situation with your bulldozer; but you DO have the power to change how it affects you.

FIELD WORK:

Examine the expectations you are putting on your bulldozer. How might they need to be adjusted?

_____

_____

_____

_____

Changing your expectations of others is not always an easy thing to do. It requires a great deal of internal examination, thought and person insight. If this is an issue you need to address, you might want to consider some personalized coaching in this area.

KEEP UP THE GOOD WORK!

I want to congratulate you for what you have accomplished during this process. As a result of your hard work, your relationships will become "new and improved"!

Throughout this process, you have:

- Taken an honest assessment of your situation, and the part you play in it,

- Become clear about what you really want and need from relationships,

- Developed a game plan to help prepare you for difficult conversations,

- Discovered how to present yourself in a more confident manner,

- And learned to effectively follow up to build on your foundation of strength.

Learning to gracefully stand up for yourself is no easy task. It takes time to learn new habits and even more so, to help others learn new habits about how you want to be treated. But you are well on your way!

Thank you for allowing me to take this journey with you. I would love to hear how this handbook has helped you, so please feel free to share your experiences with me!

You may contact me at:

Strong Tower Coaching
P.O. Box 461616
Aurora, CO 80046-1616

Email: michele@strongtowercoaching.com
Web: www.strongtowercoaching.com

One last word:

Regardless of your background or where you come from, you are worthy of happiness. You are worthy of healthy relationships. You are worthy of respect.

You are worthy of the best!